The LOST SEAL

The LOST SEAL

Words *by* Diane McKnight

Illustrations by Dorothy Emerling

MOONLIGHT PUBLISHING
LAFAYETTE, COLORADO

The Lost Seal
Text Copyright © 2006 by Diane McKnight
Illustrations Copyright © 2006 by Dorothy Emerling
Design by: F + P Graphic Design, Inc.

Printed in China.

10 9 8 7 6 5 4 3 2 1

International Standard Book Number:
ISBN 10: 0-9723422-7-3
ISBN 13: 978-0-9723422-7-8

Library of Congress Cataloging-in-Publication Data:
    McKnight, Diane M.
        The lost seal / Diane McKnight, Dorothy Emerling.
            p. cm.
        ISBN-13: 978-0-9723422-7-8
        ISBN-10: 0-9723422-7-3
     1. Weddell seal — Antarctica — McMurdo Dry Valleys.
    2. Natural history — Antarctica — McMurdo Dry Valleys.
    I. Emerling, Dorothy. II. Title.
     QL737.P64M39 2006
     599.79'6 — dc22
                                        2006000687

The mission of the Schoolyard Series is to engage children and their
families in learning about the earth's ecosystems, both locally and inter-
nationally, through narratives that reflect the dynamic research being
conducted at the National Science Foundation's Long-Term Ecological
Research Sites.

Moonlight Publishing LLC
2528 Lexington Street
Lafayette, CO 80026 USA
www.moonlight-publishing.com

Published in cooperation with the
Long-Term Ecological Research
network, which is funded by the
National Science Foundation.

To my husband Larry

and our daughters Rhea and Ariel.

—DIANE MCKNIGHT

To Paul for his steadfast support.

—DOROTHY EMERLING

Isaiah, Flossmoor, Illinois, USA.
I drew some glaciers for *The Lost Seal*. I painted some clouds going through the mountains.

Hannah, Corbridge, Northumberland, UK.
The Dry Valley has hardly any water except a few occasional streams.

Ryka, Corbridge, Northumberland, UK.
The sun is setting over the freezing Antarctic Ocean.

In Antarctica, there are cold, dry, and windy deserts all along the coast of the continent. You may think that you have to go to a warm place to find a desert, but Antarctica is home to some of the driest and most desolate deserts in the world. These deserts are unusual because there is not one cactus, snake, or any other plants and animals to be seen for miles and miles. Instead, you will see lots of dark sand and many strangely-shaped rocks.

The largest Antarctic desert is called the McMurdo Dry Valleys and is located near the northwest corner of the Ross Ice Shelf in the Transantarctic Mountains. The Transantarctic Mountains stretch across the Antarctic continent for over 2,500 miles from northern Victoria Land to Coats Land, and separate the East Antarctic Ice Sheet from the West Antarctic Ice Sheet. In some places the ice in these *ice sheets* is more than two miles thick. It is so thick that the Transantarctic Mountains appear to be almost buried by the ice.

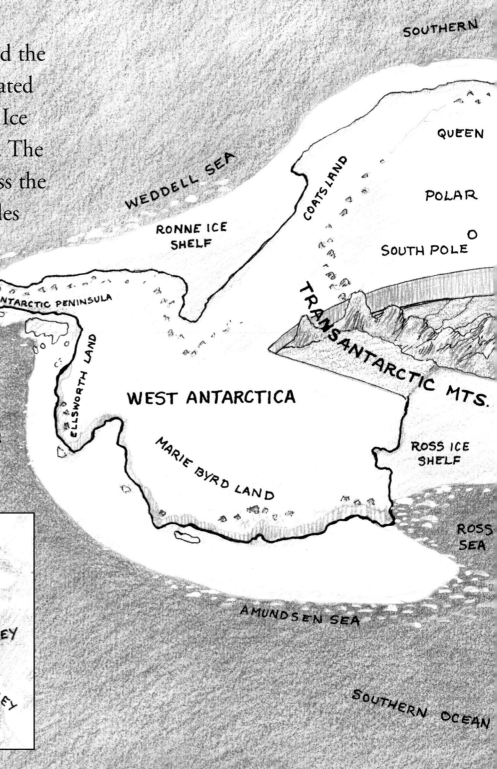

SOUTH ATLANTIC OCEAN

SOUTHERN

QUEEN

POLAR

SOUTH POLE

WEDDELL SEA

COATS LAND

RONNE ICE SHELF

ANTARCTIC PENINSULA

ELLSWORTH LAND

WEST ANTARCTICA

TRANSANTARCTIC MTS.

MARIE BYRD LAND

ROSS ICE SHELF

ROSS SEA

AMUNDSEN SEA

SOUTHERN OCEAN

SOUTH PACIFIC OCEAN

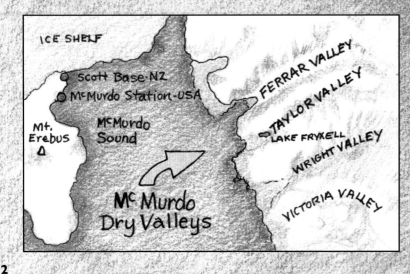

ICE SHELF

Scott Base·NZ
McMurdo Station·USA

Mt. Erebus △

McMurdo Sound

McMurdo Dry Valleys

FERRAR VALLEY

TAYLOR VALLEY

LAKE FRYXELL

WRIGHT VALLEY

VICTORIA VALLEY

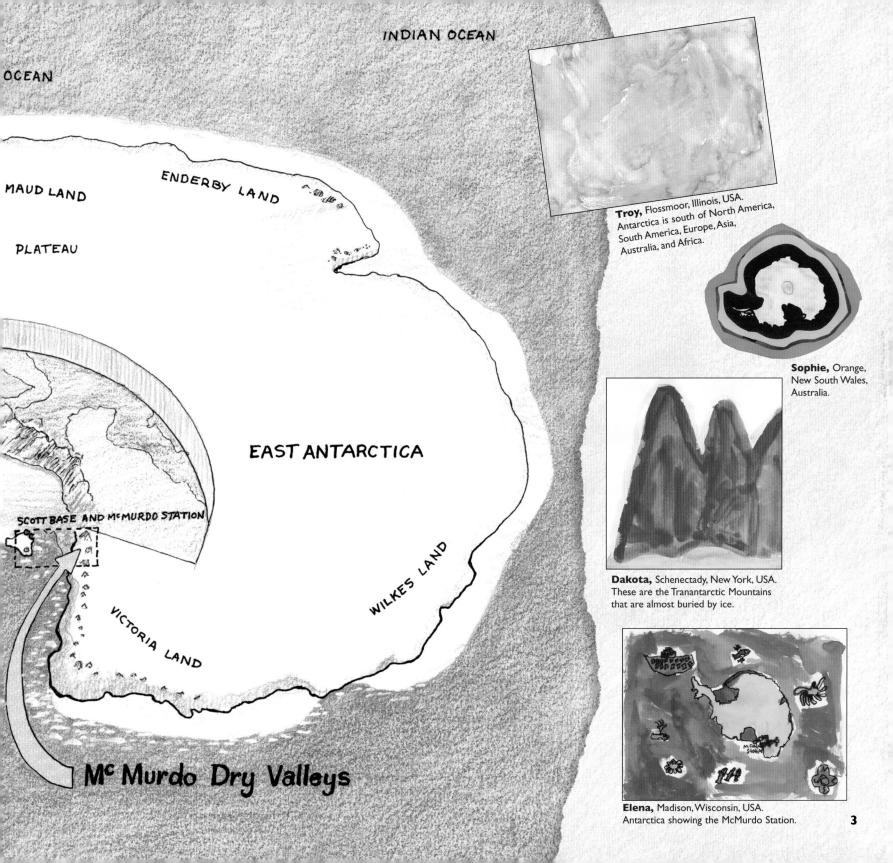

INDIAN OCEAN

OCEAN

MAUD LAND

ENDERBY LAND

PLATEAU

EAST ANTARCTICA

SCOTT BASE AND McMURDO STATION

WILKES LAND

VICTORIA LAND

McMurdo Dry Valleys

Troy, Flossmoor, Illinois, USA.
Antarctica is south of North America,
South America, Europe, Asia,
Australia, and Africa.

Sophie, Orange,
New South Wales,
Australia.

Dakota, Schenectady, New York, USA.
These are the Tranantarctic Mountains
that are almost buried by ice.

Elena, Madison, Wisconsin, USA.
Antarctica showing the McMurdo Station.

3

The McMurdo Dry Valleys were discovered in 1903 by Captain Robert Scott and two members of his Discovery expedition. They were on their way back from exploring the ice sheet, and were pulling a large sled, called a *sledge*, which held their gear and supplies. Looking for a route back to their camp at Hut Point on Ross Island, they traveled down one of the dry valleys, Taylor Valley. Captain Scott kept a journal and wrote about the Dry Valleys, describing the unusual landscape.

I cannot but think that this valley is a very wonderful place. We have seen today all the indications of colossal ice action and considerable water action, and yet neither of these agents is now at work. It is worthy of record, too, that we have seen no living thing, not even a moss or a lichen; all that we did find, far inland amongst the moraine heaps, was the skeleton of a Weddell seal, and how that came there is beyond guessing. It is certainly a valley of the dead: even the great glacier which once pushed through it has withered away.

The seal skeleton that they saw during their hike must have been one of the several *mummified* bodies of Weddell and Crabeater seals now found in Taylor Valley. These seals had crawled into the valley from their home many miles away on the sea ice and died some time ago. Scott and his men followed the dry valley, but not all the way. The valley ends in a bay, now called New Harbor, which opens onto McMurdo Sound. Later on, Scott and his men reached their camp by crossing the Sound.

Soonhyun, Madison, Wisconsin, USA.
A mummified seal in Taylor Valley. It's been there a long time.

Alkira, Leongatha, Victoria, Australia.
I really like doing pictures of animals and this is the first time I did it dead.

Katie, Columbus, Ohio, USA.
I drew a picture of Scott and his men with sleds.

5

Today, Captain Scott's *hut* can still be seen on Hut Point. Nearby is McMurdo Station, the main base for the United States Antarctic Program. Here is where scientists first arrive when they come to learn more about Antarctica. A few miles down the coast is Scott Base, the support station for the New Zealand Antarctic Program.

McMurdo Station

Scott Base

Since Scott's expedition, many scientists
have studied the lakes, streams, soils, and
glaciers of the Dry Valleys. Diane is a
member of a research team that comes to
the valleys every year. She is a *limnologist,*
a scientist who studies lakes and streams,
and she wants to understand how life sur-
vives in such a cold, hostile environment.
Captain Scott didn't notice the life in the
Dry Valleys because he didn't know where
to look. Some of the life is hidden by ice
and rocks, and some is so small that it
can only be seen using a *microscope.*

Diane's team comes to the Dry Valleys from the United States, England, New Zealand, and other countries. To get there, they take a military cargo plane from Christchurch in New Zealand to McMurdo Station. Then they travel by helicopter to the Dry Valleys. They stay in camps located on the shores of the three lakes in Taylor Valley. They sleep in backpacking tents, and they do some of their scientific work in small laboratories that are not much bigger than your bedroom.

When Diane comes back home, she is often asked, "What is it like in the Dry Valleys? What happens there?" In response, she likes to tell a true story about an amazing event that happened in 1990. On a clear, cold, sunny day in late December, when they were measuring how much water was flowing in the streams, they found much more than they ever expected. On this day, they found a seal—and it was alive!

Of course this may not seem like much to most people, but because Diane's team was so used to studying and thinking about microscopic life in the streams, finding a live seal was almost as surprising as if they had gone to the beach to collect seashells and discovered a whale stranded in the sand!

In the streams, microscopic plants, called *algae* and *bacteria* form thin mats. These mats are black and orange-brown in color, the same color as the rocks on the streambed. In the dark sandy soils, there are algae and bacteria growing on the sand grains and small curly worms, called *nematodes,* that live in a *dormant* state and only revive when there is a little bit of moisture. Even on the glaciers, algae and bacteria grow in small pockets of liquid water just under the ice, called *cryoconite holes.* The algae and bacteria that grow in the lakes are hidden under the ice, but they are very abundant. On the bottom of the lakes, *mosses* and algae form brown, spongy mats that are as thick as a sleeping bag and cover every surface.

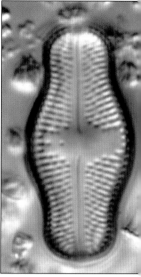

Diatom — *Luticola muticopsis*

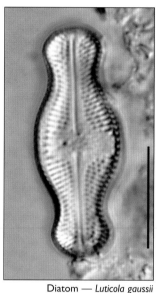

Diatom — *Luticola gaussii*

Nematode — *Scottnema*

Cryoconite hole

Bacteria from
Lake Bonney

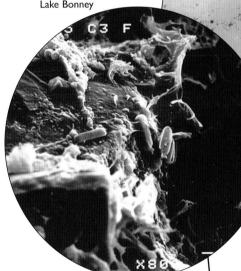

Each of the members
of Diane's research team
has many questions about the
life in the Dry Valleys. One of
Diane's questions is: "Why is the
bed of this stream covered with
algae, but there are no mats in
that stream at all?" What are
some of the things that you
observe that you wonder about?

Haley, Columbus, Ohio, USA.
I drew this picture because I was interested in
the bacteria in the Dry Valleys. In my picture is
a girl looking at bacteria.

Adam, Buckingham, Pennsylvania, USA.
Algae often look like scum on the bottom
of a pond or stream.

A few days earlier, before Diane's team found the seal, they guessed that there might be an animal in Taylor Valley when they were collecting water samples from Canada Stream. They had noticed a trail in the snow that looked as if it had been made by someone dragging a heavy bag and swinging it from side to side. It could have been another researcher, but there were no footprints! The only explanation that they could imagine was that the trail had been made by a seal. Even more puzzling was that the trail in the snow seemed to be heading up the valley towards the nearby glacier.

In the Dry Valleys, the mountains are so massive and so high that they hold back the East Antarctic Ice Sheet and keep it from reaching the ocean. The ice sheet ends in what are called **outlet glaciers** at the head of each valley. There are also small **alpine glaciers**, which spill over from the mountaintops onto the valley bottoms.

Maia, Buckingham, Pennsylvania, USA.
This is a bright blue sky, with a bright sun,
in Taylor Valley.

Karina, Pacifica, California, USA.

Nicholas, Flossmoor, Illinois, USA.
Glaciers move but you can't really see them move.
U-valleys are created by these moving glaciers and they
pick up dirt that makes moraines on the other side.

13

They told everyone back at camp of their suspicions and several days later, Dan, the camp cook, was so curious that he decided to follow the trail to see what he could find. The trail did not go in a straight line, but zigged and zagged from one patch of snow to another, and up and down the mountainside. After several hours of searching, Dan found the seal. Miraculously it was alive and eating snow! Dan came back to camp to tell the rest of the team about his discovery and they all immediately rushed off to see the seal.

When the team reached the seal, they were so excited to see the creature, but they also felt a little sad. He seemed to look tired and while he was getting water from eating the snow, they knew he must be hungry.

They also knew that they should not feed
the seal because of a law called the *Antarctic
Conservation Act,* which protects all the
animals of Antarctica from interference by
humans. Scientists who study seals and
other Antarctic wildlife are given special
permits for their research. So Diane's team
went back to camp and called the scientists
who were studying the seals in McMurdo
Sound for advice.

Amanda, Pacifica, California, USA.

Taylor, Erie, Pennsylvania, USA.
The lost seal is about to eat some snow.
He's in the Dry Valleys.

Unlike the Dry Valleys, McMurdo Sound has abundant animal life that you can't help but see. The scientists they called were studying the Weddell and Crabeater seals that live in *colonies* and dive through cracks in the sea ice to feed on the fish swimming below. Emperor and Adelie penguins also dive from the ice edge to go fishing. They raise their chicks in large colonies along the coast of Ross Island.

Emperor Penguin

Adelie Penguin

The seals and penguins are hunted by the *leopard seals* that live in McMurdo Sound, and when the sea ice breaks up in the summer, *killer whales* come to the Sound to hunt and mate.

Ryan, Cambridge, England.
My picture is about a family of penguins and their baby walking to the sea to get some food.

Killer Whale

Leopard Seal

17

The next day, three seal scientists came to the Dry Valleys. They identified the seal from the *flipper tag* on his tail flipper. They explained that the lost seal was a one-year-old male Weddell seal that had been tagged when he was a *pup.* The seal was from a colony of Weddell seals living in McMurdo Sound. They explained that it is a common, natural behavior for some young male seals to wander away from the colony looking for a new home. The scientists measured exactly how long he was, took a sample of his blood, and painted an orange stripe down his back. Because there are no colors other than blue, white, black, and brown in the Dry Valleys, the orange stripe would make it easier to find the seal. They planned to come back the next summer and look for the seal by helicopter.

Lucy, Los Angeles, California, USA.

Prue, Leongatha, Victoria, Australia.

Francesca, Tarras, Central Otago, New Zealand.

19

The seal scientists knew that the seal would not survive the winter. In the winter, it is very cold in the Dry Valleys, as cold as -40 °C—and also very dark, because the sun does not rise. Also, there are very strong winds, called *katabatic winds,* that rush down from the East Antarctic Ice Sheet, and can blow as fast as 140 miles per hour. That's really fast—like a race car!

The sand carried by these very fast winds wears down the rocks over time, making them smooth and creating strange shapes. These rocks are called *ventifacts,* which means "shaped by the wind." You might imagine that some of these rocks are shaped like bears, or sea turtles, or other wild animals, and other rocks are shaped like tables and benches and look like a fine place for a picnic.

Melanie, Columbus, Ohio, USA.
The winds in Antarctica go up to 100-140 miles per hour!

Paige, Columbus, Ohio, USA.
The Dry Valley is a desert. It has no living animals on it. In the summer it is light all day and in the winter it is dark all day.

21

Although Diane's team understood that the seal should be left to go his own way, they felt uneasy when the seal scientists left the seal and went back to McMurdo Station to continue their own research. The research team in the Dry Valleys also went back to work. In summer, the sun never sets and the average temperature is just below freezing, warm enough for the ice on the glacier surface to be melted by the sun, creating the streams that flow into the lakes.

Because there is so much ice on the lakes, it never melts away in the summer; it measures about twelve to twenty-four feet thick—that's like two or four adults standing on top of each other! Sometimes the cold meltwater from the glaciers comes rushing and roaring down the stream channels, flooding onto the lakes, but sometimes the streams are only trickles of water. Because it was a sunny day, streamflow was high and there were important measurements to be made.

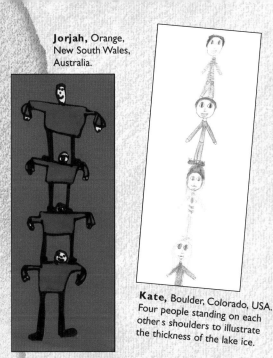

Jorjah, Orange, New South Wales, Australia.

Kate, Boulder, Colorado, USA. Four people standing on each other's shoulders to illustrate the thickness of the lake ice.

Megan, Columbus, Ohio, USA.

Harrison, Orange, New South Wales, Australia.

23

It was a few days later, and much to everyone's astonishment, when the lost seal came to the camp. A helicopter crew chief was the first one to notice his arrival. He joked that the seal must have smelled the cheeseburgers and come down the mountainside looking for food! They all knew that the camp was not a proper home for a lost, starving seal, so they called McMurdo Station again. After considering a another provision of the Antarctic Conservation Act, one that pertains to protecting human and animal life, a decision was reached to bring the lost seal back to the sea ice—his natural home.

But how was this to be done? The helicopter crew chief had a plan! He put down a *cargo net* near the seal to make a *sling load.* They placed a large piece of plywood on the net and covered it with Army blankets. Then they herded the seal onto the blankets, and strapped him down. A special wide orange rope with a loop at the end, called a *pendant,* was attached to the cargo straps and then attached to the bottom of the helicopter that hovered overhead. The helicopter lifted up the sling load and the seal was off to New Harbor on McMurdo Sound.

Rupert, Tarras, Central Otago, New Zealand.
A helicopter flies over the Antarctica Mountains.

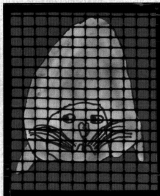

Annabelle, Orange,
New South Wales, Australia.

Sarah, Melbourne, Victoria, Australia.
This is a picture of the seal getting taken away by the helicopter

25

The flight to the edge of the sea ice lasted about ten minutes and must have been quite a ride for the seal! The pilot set the sling load down near some other Weddell seals and landed the helicopter nearby. The lost seal was so eager to get onto the sea ice that he kept pushing his head forward through the net and almost tangled himself in a knot.

When he was finally free, the seal started eating snow as fast as he could. As the helicopter took off, the research team all hoped that the lost seal would soon be catching fish under the sea ice, rather than looking for cheeseburgers back at the camp. It was quite an adventure for a research team who normally studied lakes and streams. They knew their experience with the lost seal would always be a special memory.

Andrew, Tarras, Central Otago, New Zealand.
Helicopter taking the lost seal back to its seal habitat.

Brendan, Columbus, Ohio, USA.
My watercolor is a picture of when they drop the seal off with the other seals.

Sonia, Pacifica, California, USA.

At the end of the summer, and as the research season was ending, Diane's team decided that they needed to name some of the streams they had been studying. This would help them keep track of all their measurements. Once the streams begin to flow in the summer, the researchers measure the *flow rate* for each of the major streams in Taylor Valley. They do this at *gauging stations,* where they have *instruments* that measure how deep the water is right at that spot in the stream.

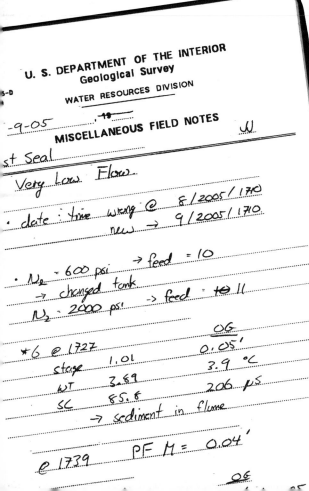

st Seal

Very Low Flow

• date : time wrong @ 8/2005/1710
                   new → 9/2005/1710

• N_2 = 600 psi → feed = 10
   → changed tank
   N_2 = 2000 psi → feed = 10 11

                    OG
*6 @ 1727   0.05'
   stage   1.01   3.9 °C
   WT   3.89   206 μS
   SC   85.8
      → sediment in flume

@ 1739   PF M = 0.04'

By knowing the water depth, they can determine how much water is flowing into the lake. It's hard to believe, but for each stream they record about 5,000 to 10,000 stream flow measurements in an eight week period every summer! When the summer is over, they add up all these measurements to determine how much water flowed into the lake from each stream.

Joanne, Columbus, Ohio, USA.

Tom, Erie, Pennsylvania, USA.
The scientists' stuff.

Gizem, Madison, Wisconsin, USA.
Four researchers studying a glacier. It's important to study glaciers.

Often when scientists study something that has not been studied before, they get the opportunity to name it. Just like the rules that govern interaction with Antarctic animals, there are specific rules for naming places in Antarctica. Names can be chosen to describe some aspect of the place itself, to honor the people who have worked there, who have advanced science in some way, or to commemorate an event that has happened there.

Since some of the Taylor Valley streams did not have names, the scientists were thrilled to have the chance to name them. So with much enthusiasm, and a unanimous vote, they chose to name one of the major streams that flows into Lake Fryxell: Lost Seal Stream.

It is a name that not only commemorates the long, hard journey of a young seal, but also celebrates the first recorded encounter of humans and a live seal in the polar desert of the Dry Valleys. Today, anyone visiting those valleys in Antarctica might not see any seals, but they would be able to find Lost Seal Stream and imagine the adventure of one young Weddell seal.

Chelsea, Leongatha, Victoria, Australia. My painting is about a sunset with three hills with snow on them. It also has a penguin sliding down the hill.

Amy, Arbury, Cambridge, England. This picture is a sunset. It has a mountain and some water in it. It looks so peaceful.

LOST SEAL STREAM

COMMONWEALTH GLACIER

LOST SEAL STREAM

HUEY CREEK

NORTH

FRYXELL CAMP

LAKE FRYXELL

CANADA STREAM

CANADA GLACIER

CRESCENT STREAM

HARNISH STREAM

McKNIGHT CREEK

AIKEN CREEK

VON GUERARD STREAM

Glossary

algae—Plants that grow in water and do not have stems, roots or leaves; many are only one cell and are too small to be seen without a microscope.

alpine glaciers—Glaciers located in mountains.

Antarctic Conservation Act—A federal law that protects animals and plants in Antarctica.

bacteria—Organisms that are only one cell, do not have a true nucleus, and are too small to be seen without a microscope.

cargo net—A net made of three-inch-wide cloth strips used for packing supplies.

colonies—a group of animals living together in a small area.

cryoconite hole—a shallow hole in the ice on the surface of a glacier containing water and sediment.

dormant—Alive, but not growing.

flipper tag—A piece of plastic attached to a seal for identification.

flow rate—The amount of water moving past a point in a stream in a period of time.

gauging stations—A place in a stream where instruments are set up to measure flow rate.

glaciers—Large masses of ice that last for many years.

hut—A small building used as a shelter from harsh conditions.

ice sheets—Very large glaciers that cover a continent.

instruments—Devices designed for a special use, such as measuring flow rate.

katabatic winds—Strong warm winds that come down from ice sheets.

killer whales—Small whales with white patches on their backs; another name for a killer whale is an Orca.

leopard seals—Large predatory seals that have a spotted coat.

limnologist—A scientist who studies lakes and streams.

microscope—A magnifying device that allows extremely small things to be seen.

mosses—Tiny-leaved flowerless plants that grow in moist places.

mummified—Preserved by being dried out.

nematodes—Small worms that mainly live in soil.

outlet glaciers—Glaciers that come from an ice sheet.

pendant—A thick rope with a loop on one end.

pup—A baby seal.

sledge—A large sled used for hauling gear.

sling load—Cargo wrapped up in a net carried underneath a helicopter.

ventifacts—Rocks that have been smoothed and polished over many years by sand blown in the wind.

Acknowledgments

This book was prepared in recognition of the International Polar Year (2007-2008) by scientists of the McMurdo Dry Valleys Long-Term Ecological Research project, located at the Institute of Arctic and Alpine Research, University of Colorado, and the Byrd Polar Research Center, The Ohio State University. Support for the book was provided by the Schoolyard Program of the Long-Term Ecological Research Program of the National Science Foundation (grant numbers OPP-9810219 and OPP-0423595).

The book includes text and illustrations contributed by students in elementary classes in Australia, England, New Zealand, and the United States as part of their studies of the Antarctic, which included viewing the video of the seal taken at the time of this event. The publisher, author, and illustrator would like to thank the following organizations, schools, and individuals for participating in the preparation of this book.

Organizations
- Antarctica New Zealand
- Australian Antarctic Division
- British Antarctic Survey
- International Polar Foundation
- National Science Foundation

Participating Schools
- Arbury Primary School, Carton Way, Cambridge, UK; teacher-Diane Rawlings
- Bixby School, Boulder, CO, USA; teacher-Robert MacKenzie
- Bluffsview Elementary School, Columbus, OH, USA; teachers-Donna Gehring, Becky Grabosky and Kathy Westbrook
- Corbridge Middle School, Northumberland, UK; teacher-Emma Clarke
- Creative Environment Day School, Fayetteville, NY, USA; teacher-Kimberly Taylor
- Flossmoor Montessori School, Flossmoor, IL, USA; teacher-Shawn Manner
- Buckingham Elementary School, Buckingham, PA, USA; teacher-Eileen Koch
- Belle Valley School, Erie, PA, USA; teacher-Glenn McKnight

- Granby Elementary School, Columbus, OH, USA; teachers-Michelle Harper and Todd Korn
- King's Highway Elementary School, Clearwater, FL, USA; teacher-Cynthia Melendez
- Kinross Wolaroi Preparatory School, Orange, NSW, Australia; teacher-Rebecca Whiteley
- Lee St. Primary School, Carlton North, Victoria, Australia; teacher-Anne Bleeser
- Leongatha Primary School, Victoria, Australia; teacher-Marg Callanan
- Liberty Elementary School, Columbus, OH, USA; teachers-Linda Lehman and Sandy Downie
- Margate Primary School, Tasmania, Australia; teacher-Roger O'Meagher
- New South Wales Primary School, Yarramundi, NSW, Australia; teacher-Lauren Broos
- Ocean Shore School, Pacifica, CA, USA; teacher-Des Garner
- Shorewood Elementary School, Madison, WI, USA; teacher-Erica Smith
- Tarras School, Central Otago, New Zealand; teacher-Nicki Crabbe

Individuals
- Emma Broos, Sydney, Australia
- Linda Capper, British Antarctic Survey, UK
- Karen Cozzetto, University of Colorado, Boulder, CO, USA
- Jake Croall, Hamilton, New Zealand
- Peter Doran, University of Illinois-Chicago, Chicago, USA
- Andrew Fountain, Portland State University, Portland, OR, USA
- Christopher Gardner, The Ohio State University, Columbus, OH, USA
- Chris and Vivien Hendy, Hamilton, New Zealand
- Alison Hume, Alison's Kids Antarctic Art Project, Australia
- Jean Janecki, University of Wisconsin-Madison, Madison, WI, USA
- Nadene Kennedy, U.S. National Science Foundation, Arlington, VA, USA
- Carol Landis, The Ohio State University, Columbus, OH, USA
- W.B. Lyons, The Ohio State University, Columbus, OH, USA
- Carolyn McKnight, Los Angeles, CA, USA
- Glenna McKnight, Manlius, NY, USA

- Claudia Mills, University of Colorado, Boulder, CO, USA
- Jean de Pomereu, International Polar Foundation
- John Priscu, Montana State University, Bozeman, MT, USA
- Emma Reid, Antarctica New Zealand
- Ursula Ryan, Antarctica New Zealand
- Shelly Sommer, University of Colorado, Boulder, CO, USA
- Brent Stewart, Hubbs-SeaWorld Research Institute, San Diego, CA, USA
- Brian Stone, U.S. National Science Foundation, Arlington, VA, USA
- Donna Sutherland, National Institute of Water and Atmospheric Research, Christchurch, New Zealand
- Bruce Tate, British Antarctic Survey, UK
- Ward Testa, U.S. National Oceanic and Atmospheric Administration, Anchorage, AK, USA
- Martyn Tranter, University of Bristol, UK
- Penny Tranter, Bath, UK
- Diana Wall, Colorado State University, Fort Collins, CO, USA
- Terry Wilson, The Ohio State University, Columbus, OH, USA

About the Long Term Ecological Research Network

The National Science Foundation's LTER network was begun in 1980 and now (2006) includes 26 research sites (http://www.lternet.edu/). The goals of the LTER network are:

- **Understanding:** To understand a diverse array of ecosystems at multiple spatial and temporal scales.

- **Synthesis:** To create general knowledge through long-term, interdisciplinary research, synthesis of information, and development of theory.

- **Information:** To inform the LTER and broader scientific community by creating well-designed and well-documented databases.

- **Legacies:** To create a legacy of well-designed and documented long-term observations, experiments, and archives of samples and specimens for future generations.

- **Education:** To promote training, teaching, and learning about long-term ecological research and the Earth's ecosystems, and to educate a new generation of scientists.

- **Outreach:** To reach out to the broader scientific community, natural resource managers, policymakers, and the general public by providing decision support, information, recommendations, and the knowledge and capability to address complex environmental challenges

The Schoolyard Series is one component of a broad-scale, long-term effort to combine scientific research and science education through the Schoolyard LTER program (http://schoolyard.lternet.edu/).

The LTER network in the United States is joined with similar research networks of scientists in at least 30 other countries through the International Long Term Ecological Research (ILTER) network (http://www.ilternet.edu/). The scientists in the ILTER are collectively engaged and dedicated to multi- and interdisciplinary long-term and large spatial scale research and monitoring in ecological science.

The Lost Seal Website (http://www.mcmlter.org/lostseal/) presents artwork contributed by all the children in the participating classrooms. The website includes video clips of the lost seal, the field camp and a visiting penguin filmed at the time, as well as photographs from the McMurdo Dry Valleys.